Sneakers ABC's™
of
State Park
Activities

A guide for kids to Park programs and activities

by Sally Jones, Jackie Fergestad and Carol Amundson

illustrated by Jackie Fergestad

This book is a celebration of long and lasting friendships
and dear and loving families.

Other **Sneakers ABCs**™ books:

Sneakers ABCs – a guidebook to Minneapolis Park Activities

Sneakers ABCs - a guidebook to Rochester Park Activities

Ryan Raccoon

DNR

Minnesota State Parks

Lily Loon

Sneakers

Sally

Sneakers and Sally join new State Park friends. Come on their adventures and see where they end!

1

Afton State Park

It's **A**utumn in the **A**rrowhead.

The **A**rtists like to draw it.

There are **A**nglers by the lakeshore,

Sneakers' **A**rrow hits his target!

B

Banning   Big Stone Lake
Bear Head Lake   Blue Mounds
Beaver Creek Valley   Buffalo River

Sneakers chases

Butterflies.

He has to jump and run.

Bears and Beavers,

Birds and Bugs

are watching him have fun!

Camden
Cascade River
Charles A. Lindbergh

Crow Wing
Cuyuna Country

Caves, Canoes and Cookout fires, Cameras and Coolers, too; a Compass for the hiking trail; Camping's fun to do!

Canoes • Cookout • Cameras • Coolers • Compass • Camping • Climbing • Cemeteries

Cross-Country skiing • Cabins • Cartography • Collecting • Caves • Cascade

On a **D**riving **D**ay trip,
count the Park **D**elights -
from **D**ucks and **D**ogs
and spotted **D**eer
to **D**ragonflies in flight!

8

Deciduous • Discover • Dandelions • Digging • Dams • Day trips • Dragonflies • Dogs

Danger • Drive • Deer • Does • Ducks • DNR • Douglas Lodge

The trails at
Eagle Mountain
are **E**xciting to **E**xplore.

Once we reach the tippy top
we can see the **E**agles soar!

EXPERT TRAIL

EAGLE MT.
Highest Point in
Minnesota

The Forest Ranger
at the Falls
can see from Fort to Fort.
From Fishing to
Four-wheeling,
he's quite an active sport!

Hike the Gitchi Gummi Trail and spot a Great Horned Owl. Listen to Gooseberry Falls or hear the Grey wolves howl!

Garden Island
Glacial Lakes
Glendalough
Great River Bluffs

George Crosby-Manitou
Gooseberry Falls
Grand Portage

14

Groundhogs • Gophers • Gardens • Growl • Gnats • Grasshoppers • Geese • Grouse

GOOSEBERRY FALLS

Great Horned Owl • Golden Eagles • Grandparents • Gloves • Golf • Glacier

15

Hayes Lake
Hill Annex Mine

Ryan likes the Headwaters.

He sings a Happy tune.

His friend has brought

a Hat along,

it must be Lily Loon!

Interstate
Itasca

Minnesota Winter is

Ice fishing on a lake,

building a snow Igloo,

or learning how to skate!

Jay Cooke
John A. Latsch
Judge C. R. Magney

Join the frogs at **J**ay Cooke Park!

They're going for a **J**og!

Sally takes the long way 'round while Sneakers

Jumps the log!

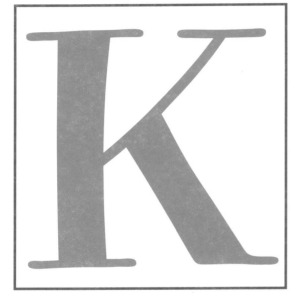

Kilen Woods

Big **K**ids learn to

Kayak.

It really takes a **K**nack

to ride the river rapids

and then to paddle back!

Kayaking • Knapsack • Knife • Kerchief • Kiosk • Khakis • Kingfisher • Kids • map Key

Kindling • Kid-friendly • King Snakes • Knots • Knowledge • Kilometer

23

Lac Qui Parle   Lake Louise
Lake Bemidji   Lake Maria
Lake Bronson   Lake Shetek
Lake Carlos

There's a Lighthouse

they call Split Rock,

Lily leads the way.

"Don't forget your Life vest,

the Lake is rough today!"

Maplewood
McCarthy Beach
Mille Lacs-Kathio
Minneopa

Minnesota Valley
Monson Lake
Moose Lake
Myre-Big Island

The friends biked Miles and Miles today and now it's time to rest— with Music and a roaring fire, toasted Marshmallows are best!

Nerstrand Big Woods

Maple trees show us Spring
is near along the
great North Shore.
A Naturalist can tell us
how to
make the syrup pour!

Old Mill

"Orienteering" is a word

for following a map.

Ryan brings a walking

stick, a compass and a cap.

SCENIC OVERL**OO**K

OBSERVATION POINT

OUTWARD BOUND

R

MAP

31

Paul Bunyan is the
Pineland King
with Babe, his faithful ox.
Jam and Peanut butter
fill up the Picnic box!

32

Park Pals • Photography • Portages • Predators • Pop-up tents • Paddling • Poaching

Prairie Dogs • Pebbles • Pyrite • Pheasants • Poison Ivy • Porcupines • Paths

It's Quiet at the Quarry.

Sally spots a Quail.

She finds a pretty

piece of Quartz

but leaves it by the trail.

Quails • Quiet time • Questions • Quarry • Quills • Quartz • Quality activities

"Quacking" • Quick thinking • Quivers • Queues (lines)

Red Lake
Red River
Rice Lake

Ryan's in his Rain gear
fishing in the River.
The Rabbits all are hiding
'cuz the Raindrops
make them shiver!

S

Sneakers likes to Snowmobile,
Sally likes her Skis.
This Season they will
both have fun
in Snow up to their knees.

Snow • Swimming • Spelunking • Skiing • Shrews • Sunfish • Skunks • Sleeping bags

Spear fishing • Sounds • Seasonal • Snowshoing • See-saws • Squirrels • Smelt

39

Temperance River
Tettegouche

Sneakers takes his Telescope to Travel to the stars. When the night is clear enough he can see the planet Mars!

Upper Sioux Agency

At the Underground mine

near the town of Soudan

the guide will explain

how the ore cars ran!

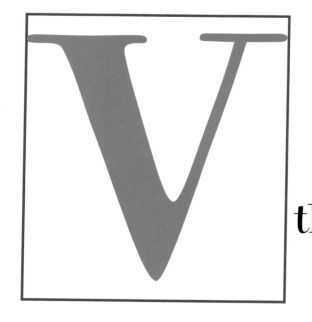

Lily Loon is a Park **V**olunteer.
She helps the **V**isitors see
the **V**ariety each Park offers
and guides folks
through history!

Volunteers • Visitors • Villages • Vehicles • Vultures • Vacation • Variety • Vegetation

Voyageurs • Vouchers • Viceroy butterflies • Volunteers • Visitors • Vacation

45

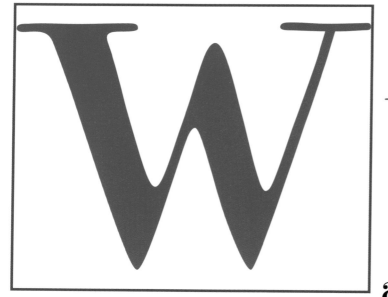

Whitewater
Wild River
William O'Brien

Sally and Lily are Whispering as they Wander in the Wood. They spot a Weasel and a White-tailed deer as only Park Pals could!

46

eXtra! eXtra!

Come to the Fair!

The State Park eXhibits

have so much to share!

eXcitement • "X" marks the spot on the map • eXperiences • eXhilaration

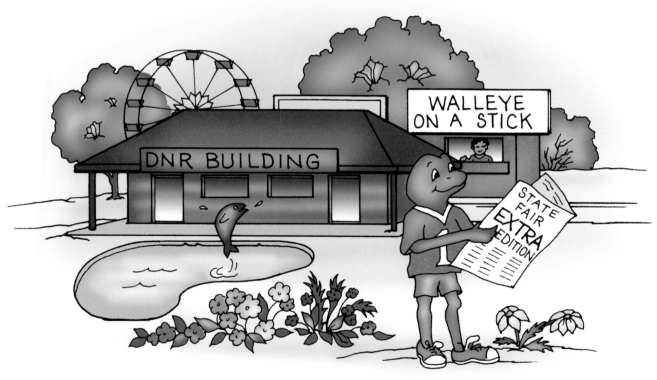

eXercise • eXamine • eXit • Hill AnneX Mine State Park

The Youngsters are in

Yellow,

Yawning very wide.

They got up extra early

to watch the big moose hide.

Zippel Bay

52

We've **Z**ipped across the grasslands,

we've toured State Parks with **Z**est,

Zig-**Z**agged up and down the trails,

Minnesota Parks are best!

Zoological • Zoom • Zigzag trails • Zest & Zeal • Zephyrs • wildlife Zones

"Join us for fun in the Minnesota State Parks!"

53

Minnesota State Parks

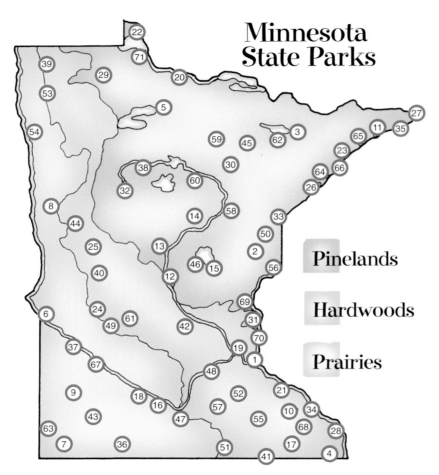

Pinelands

Hardwoods

Prairies

1 Afton 651-436-5391
2 Banning 320-245-2668
3 Bear Head Lake 218-365-7229
4 Beaver Creek Valley 507-724-2107
5 Big Bog State Recreation Area
   (under development)
6 Big Stone Lake 320-839-3663
7 Blue Mounds 507-283-1307
8 Buffalo River 218-498-2124
9 Camden 507-865-4530
10 Carley c/o Whitewater
   507-932-3007
11 Cascade River 218-387-3053
12 Charles A. Lindbergh 320-616-2525
13 Crow Wing 218-829-8022
14 Cuyuna Country Recreation Area
   320-546-5926
15 Father Hennepin 320-676-8763
16 Flandrau 507-233-9800
17 Forestville / Mystery Cave Park
   507-352-5111, Cave: 507-937-3251
18 Fort Ridgely 507-426-7840
19 Fort Snelling 612-725-2389

20 Franz Jevne c/o Zippel Bay
    218-783-6252
21 Frontenac 651-345-3401
22 Garden Island State Recreation
    Area c/o Zippel Bay
    218-783-6252
23 George H. Crosby-Manitou c/o
    Tettegouche 218-226-6365
24 Glacial Lakes 320-239-2860
25 Glendalough 218-864-0110
26 Gooseberry Falls 218-834-3855
27 Grand Portage 218-475-2360
28 Great River Bluffs 507-643-6849
29 Hayes Lake 218-425-7504
30 Hill Annex Mine 218-247-7215
31 Interstate 651-465-5711
32 Itasca 218-266-2100
33 Jay Cooke 218-384-4610
34 John A. Latsch c/o Whitewater
    507-932-3007
35 Judge C.R. Magney 218-387-3039
36 Kilen Woods 507-662-6258
37 Lac qui Parle 320-752-4736

38 Lake Bemidji 218-755-3843
39 Lake Bronson 218-754-2200
40 Lake Carlos 320-852-7200
41 Lake Louise 507-324-5249
42 Lake Maria 763-878-2325
43 Lake Shetek 507-763-3256
44 Maplewood 218-863-8383
45 McCarthy Beach 218-254-2411
46 Mille Lacs-Kathio 320-532-3524
47 Minneopa 507-389-5464
48 Minnesota Valley Recreation Area
    952-492-6400
49 Monson Lake 320-366-3797
50 Moose Lake 218-485-5420
51 Myre-Big Island 507-379-3403
52 Nerstrand Big Woods
    507-334-8848
53 Old Mill 218-437-8174
54 Red River State Recreation Area
    (under development)
55 Rice Lake 507-455-5871
56 St. Croix 320-384-6591
57 Sakatah Lake 507-362-4438

58 Savanna Portage 218-426-3271
59 Scenic 218-743-3362
60 Schoolcraft c/o Hill Annex
    218-247-7215
61 Sibley 320-354-2055
62 Soudan Underground Mine
    218-753-2245
63 Split Rock Creek 507-348-7908
64 Split Rock Lighthouse
    218-226-6377
65 Temperance River 218-663-7476
66 Tettegouche 218-226-6365
67 Upper Sioux Agency 320-564-4777
68 Whitewater 507-932-3007
69 Wild River 651-583-2125
70 William O'Brien 651-433-0500
71 Zippel Bay 218-783-6252

Web site: www.dnr.state.mn.us

55

Minnesota State Park Trivia Quiz

1. Which is Minnesota's largest state park?

2. Which park is nicknamed Little Itasca?

3. How many state parks have the word Lake, River or Creek in their title?

4. How many state parks have waterfalls?

5. Which state park has the tallest waterfall?

6. Which is the oldest state Park?

7. Which state park has 8 major lakes within its 9,250 acres?

8. Lake Itasca is the headwaters of the Mississippi River. How long is this river?

9. Larson's Old Flour Mill was located in which park?

10. The Minnesota River starts in which state park?

11. Which state park was the site of the U.S. - Dakota Indian Conflict?

12. Which five state parks have lookout towers you can climb?

13. The historic Douglas Lodge is located in which park?

14. The WPA built a stone bridge in Split Rock Creek State Park in which year?

15. How many state parks are home to a major historical site?

16. Our state parks are divided into how many ecological regions?

17. The Mississippi and the Minnesota Rivers converge in which state park?

18. Which is the smallest Minnesota state park?

19. Which state park has the most annual visitors?

Places of special interest in Minnesota

Split Rock Lighthouse—a 1910 beacon perched above Lake Superior

Soudan Underground Mine—an iron ore mine far below the earth's surface

Historic Forestville—1899 village brings memories back to life

Charles A. Lindbergh—aviator's home and museum

Mille Lacs-Kathio—100 foot observation tower, can be climbed to the top

Hill Annex Mine—open pit mine, was one of the nation's richest

Larson's Flour Mill & Log Cabin—this historic site became Old Mill State Park

Shetek Settlers Monument & Koch Cabin—located in Lake Shetek State Park

Hambrecht Historical Cottage & Museum—open weekends at Lake Louise State Park

Safety Education Programs offered by the Minnesota State Park System:

a. Advanced Hunter Education

b. Bow Hunter Education

c. Firearms Safety

d. Boat and Water Safety

e. Recreational Vehicle Safety

f. Snowmobile Safety

Trivia Quiz Answers

1. St. Croix has over 34,000 acres.
2. Schoolcraft
3. 23
4. 10
5. Grand Portage
6. Itasca, established in 1891
7. Maplewood
8. 2,552 miles
9. Old Mill
10. Big Stone Lake
11. Fort Ridgley
12. Kilen Woods, Lake Bronson, Mille Lacs-Kathio, Scenic, St. Croix
13. Lake Itasca
14. 1937
15. 36
16. 3: Pinelands, Hardwoods, Prairies
17. Fort Snelling
18. Franz Jevne
19. Fort Snelling: 700,000
    Gooseberry Falls: 580,360

57

Recommended Equipment for visiting the State Parks

Daytrips:

Appropriate sporting equipment

Good walking shoes

Long pants for walking in the woods

Water bottle

Small First-Aid kit

Insect repellent

Sunscreen

Flashlight

Camera and film

Moistened towel in a plastic bag

Hat

Large handerchief

Prescription medicines

Camping:

•Tenting: Ground cloth

　　　　　Air mattress or pad

　　　　　Sleeping bag or blankets

•General: Cook stove or firewood (check State Park

　　　　　burning rules)

　　　　　Cooking utensils, soap, dishpan

　　　　　First-aid kit

　　　　　Cooler with tight lid, ice

　　　　　Tool kit, disposable lighter

　　　　　Towels (paper and shower)

　　　　　Toilet paper, hand soap

　　　　　Trash bags

　　　　　Large water jug

　　　　　Food resistant to spoilage and in airtight,

　　　　　bugproof containers

　　　　　Walkie-talkies

　　　　　Rain gear

•Items from Daytrip list

Day Hiker's Basic Equipment

Hiking boots	Hat	Knife	Snack
Wool socks	Bandana	Signal whistle	Insect repellent
Lightweight pants or shorts	Binoculars	Sunscreen	First-aid kit
	Camera	Water bottle	Poncho
Long Sleeved Shirt	Belly pack or day pack	Hiking stick	

- When Camping in a State Park make sure that you know the rules and regulations for reservations, vehicles, exploration, etc.

- Have a pocket guide handy that identifies poisonous plants if you are not absolutely sure what they look like.

- Try to have a map of the area you are visiting.

- Cell phones are handy, but there is not always reception available in remote State Park areas, so please remember to let someone know where the area is that you will be camping or exploring, when you expect to return home and carry identification and emergency information on your person. If you are new to a Park area, register with the Park Office that you are a visitor and unfamiliar with the trails, etc.

- Keep your children safe. It is so easy for children to get excited about something and go racing off. It only takes a second for them to be gone. Talk about staying together, agree on a plan of what to do if you are ever separated and make sure they understand how important it is to follow that plan! It is also a good idea for each child to carry a small identification card with emergency information, whom to contact, and any appropriate health information.

Have you seen . . . ?

This is some of the wildlife that can be found in Minnesota's State Parks:

Badgers	Bobcats	Fox	Moose	Squirrels
Bald Eagles	Chipmunks	Geese	Owls	Vultures
Bats	Cougar	Grouse	Otters	White Pelicans
Beaver	Coyotes	Hawks	Porcupines	Wild Turkey
Bison	Deer	Loons	Rabbits	Wolves
Black Bear	Elk	Lynx	Raccoons	Woodchucks
Birds of all kinds	Fish of all kinds	Mice	Skunks	and much more . . .

Minnesota State Parks are home to . . .

Banning Sandstone Quarry	Lakes	Prairies
Creeks	Lighthouse	Rivers
Grasslands	Log Cabins	Scenic Vistas
Glacial Beds	Marshes	Stone Bridges
Hardwood Forests	Mystery Cave	Streams
Headwaters of the Mississippi	Old Flour Mill	Underground Iron Ore Mine
Rivers	Open Pit Mine	Waterfalls
Historic Forts	Pinelands	Woodlands
Indian Mounds	Pioneer Cemetery	
Islands	Pioneer Town Sites	

Minnesota Favorites

State Bird: Loon
State Tree: Norway Pine
State Song: "Hail Minnesota"
State Butterfly: Monarch

State Fish: Walleye
State Mushroom: Morel
State Grain: Wild Rice
State Muffin: Blueberry

State Drink: Milk
State Gemstone: Lake Superior Agate
State Flower: Pink and White
Lady Slipper

About the Authors

Sally Jones, Jackie Fergestad, and Carol Amundson have enjoyed a long and lasting friendship since their days at Minneapolis Washburn High School, Class of '66. They formed Sneakers & Company LLC to publish the Sneakers' ABCs series of books to encourage kids to experience Park activities.

Sneakers & Company LLC creates customized commissioned editions for state or local agencies.
For information e-mail: sneakerscompany@aol.com

Abundant thanks for your support!

Rod Amundson
Dan Breva

Ruth Christianson
Jim Fergestad
Nancy and Gordy Shonka

Karen Hassett
Bill Jacobs

61

This is a special gift for

_____

from

_____